BENEATH THE SURFACE

MEMORIES OF A SURGEON

DR AKSHAY HANAMSHETTI

Made with ♥ on the Notion Press Platform
www.notionpress.com

To my mom and dad,
For your unconditional love, sacrifices, and the values that
shaped who I am today.

To my sister, Akshata,
For being my unwavering support and my constant source
of strength.

And to my wife, Shrusti,
For your endless patience, love, and belief in me, even
during the longest days and sleepless nights.

This book is for you all—my foundation, my inspiration,
my everything.

Contents

Preface

When I first set foot in the operating room, I thought I knew what it meant to be a surgeon. The years of study, the relentless exams, the hours spent perfecting techniques—all of it felt like preparation for this role. But nothing prepared me for the truth: that surgery is a profession defined not by certainty but by its constant proximity to doubt.

As a young surgeon, you quickly realize that every decision matters, that your hands carry not just the responsibility of skill but the weight of trust. There is no room for hesitation, yet you feel it creeping in at every turn. The patient on the table doesn't see the conflict within you, the tension between what you know and what you hope.

This book is not a celebration of expertise or a chronicle of perfection. It is an honest account of the challenges faced by someone still early in their journey—a surgeon learning not only how to save lives but also how to accept failure, to grapple with imperfection, and to keep going despite the weight of it all.

The stories in Beneath the Surface are drawn from those first years, when every case teaches you something new, not just about medicine but about yourself. It's a reflection on the humanity of this profession: the patients who trust us, the colleagues who guide us, and the moments that remind us why we chose this path. For all its challenges, surgery is, at its heart, a privilege—one I'm still learning to deserve.

Prologue

The first time I held a scalpel, my hands trembled. It wasn't fear, exactly—more like the weight of the moment pressing against my palms. I was about to make the first cut into another human being, a stranger who had placed their trust in me without knowing who I was or what I was capable of.

In medical school, they teach you anatomy in neat diagrams and labeled parts, as if the body were a machine. But nothing prepares you for the warmth of living tissue, the resistance of muscle beneath the blade, or the unspoken responsibility that hums in the air of an operating room.

Surgery is supposed to be clinical, methodical, precise. Yet, it is also profoundly human. Each patient who lies on the table is more than just a case or a diagnosis. They bring with them their fears, their hopes, their lives—messy, complex, and fragile. And when you stand at the crossroads of their vulnerability and your skill, the line between healer and human becomes impossibly thin.

I've spent years learning the art of surgery, and even longer learning the art of being a doctor. But what they don't tell you is that, in this profession, every scar you leave on someone else leaves a mark on you, too.

This is a story of those marks—of the moments that have shaped me, challenged me, and sometimes broken me. It is a story of the people who trusted me with their lives and the lessons they taught me in return.

Though the names and places in this story have been changed, the essence of these events remains true. These are the experiences that have shaped me, challenged me,

and, in some ways, saved me.
Welcome to the world beneath the surface.

CHAPTER ONE

THE MODERN SURGEON

In the quiet hum of a hospital corridor, the modern physician walks a tightrope between worlds. One foot grounded in the traditions of medicine — in the ancient art of diagnosis, of touch, of intuition — the other foot stepping cautiously, sometimes clumsily, into the ever-quickening current of technological change. They are an embodiment of contrasts: figures of calm precision in a setting where beeping monitors, blinking lights, and the quiet panic of waiting families swirl relentlessly.

The tools they wield today are marvels — sharp, sleek, and cold. A scalpel has become a laser; a careful incision replaced by an intricate dance of robotic arms guided by human hands. Where once there was certainty in the tactile, the audible — the rasp of diseased tissue beneath gloved fingers, the subtle variations of breath — there is now an ocean of data. A screen showing countless variables, probabilities, and suggested pathways. The modern physician must be a navigator of this digital sea, but the compass remains stubbornly human.

They wear the uniform of their trade, though even this has evolved. The pristine white coat — a symbol of authority, of cleanliness, of distance — still lingers in clinics and corridors, but it now flaps open to reveal scrubs dyed in cheerful hues, adorned with whimsical patterns. Perhaps these colors are an unconscious defense against the starkness of the work, a way to soften the sharp edges of reality. And atop their heads, a strange assembly: magnifying loupes, lights, headgear that looks more fitting for a machinist or a miner. The irony is clear — in their quest for precision, they become almost comically encumbered.

But the humor is fleeting.

Because beneath the gadgets and the jargon, there is still the weight of responsibility. They carry this weight quietly, aware that technology, no matter how advanced, cannot absolve them of failure. If anything, it makes failure harder to forgive. A misdiagnosis, a missed cue, or a lapse in judgment remains painfully human. And the knowledge that they are fallible — that beneath the sterile veneer of modern medicine lies the old, frail truth of human limitation — gnaws quietly at the edges of their resolve.

In the operating theater, amid the glow of monitors and the soft whirr of machinery, the modern physician performs with a kind of detached intimacy. The instruments extend their hands, magnify their eyes, refine their movements. They manipulate robotic arms with the delicacy of a puppeteer, yet they are never fully removed. The sweat that prickles at the nape of their neck, the subtle shift in breath when a complication arises — these are the irreducible signs that a human is still at the helm. Technology is a tool, but it is not the surgeon.

Their language, too, reflects this duality. They speak of "laparoscopic resection," of "endovascular repair," of "robot-assisted procedures" — words that sound cold, clinical, safe. Yet when they turn to the patient or the patient's family, their vocabulary shrinks. It becomes simple, deliberate: "We did everything we could." Sometimes, it reduces to silence. A hand on a shoulder. A nod. An admission that medicine, for all its advancements, still fails more often than we like to admit.

Between procedures, they step into hallways, juggling messages, emails, and digital charts. Their phone vibrates with notifications — a patient's lab results, an urgent consult, an update from a colleague on the other side of the world. There is no pause, no respite. They sip coffee that has gone cold, bite into a granola bar that tastes of cardboard and exhaustion. They wonder, fleetingly, if they are keeping up, if they can continue to bear the demands of this new world — a world where medicine never sleeps and, therefore, neither do they.

And yet, they stay.

They stay because, beneath the layers of technology and the weight of expectations, there remains the simple, stubborn desire to help. To alleviate suffering, to restore dignity, to bear witness to the fragility of life and, in some small way, to mend it. The same desire that drove their predecessors — those physicians who worked by the dim light of kerosene lamps, who relied on intuition honed by experience rather than algorithms — still burns within them.

The modern physician is not so different, after all. They are not defined by the tools they use, but by the choices they make. To show up, to try again, to hold onto the quiet belief that what they do matters. The laser, the robot, the data — these are just instruments. The essence of their work, and their humanity, remains unchanged.

And as they glance toward the future — toward a generation of physicians who will undoubtedly master technologies still unimaginable — they feel a quiet hope. Not that the future will be easier, but that it will still be human. That no matter how advanced medicine becomes, the heart of it will remain the same: one human, standing beside another, saying, "I will help you."

CHAPTER TWO

THE ANATOMY OF GRIEF

It wasn't supposed to happen. Not to this patient, not under my care.

The operation was routine—a simple fixation for a femoral fracture in an elderly woman. She'd fallen in her kitchen, slipping on a patch of spilled water, her brittle bones no match for the sudden impact. Her son, a young man with a face still soft with boyish worry, had held her hand as they wheeled her into pre-op. "She's a fighter, Doctor," he'd said, his voice trembling. "She's been through worse."

I had reassured him with the same steady words I'd said to so many others. "We'll take good care of her. She's in safe hands."

The surgery went smoothly. Her bones came together with textbook precision, the plate and screws fitting neatly into place. I remember stepping back from the table, feeling that quiet satisfaction that comes when things go exactly as planned.

And then, just as we were closing, her blood pressure began to drop.

At first, it was subtle—just a slight dip on the monitor. The anesthetist adjusted the fluids, her calm voice barely registering in the hum of the machines. But the numbers continued to fall, slow at first, then precipitously. A cascade of events unfolded in minutes: the oxygen levels plummeted, her heart faltered, and the room, which had been filled with routine chatter, became unbearably silent. We worked frantically, calling for emergency drugs, checking and rechecking lines, searching for an explanation. A clot, perhaps? A sudden embolism? The possibilities raced through my mind, each one worse than the last.

And then it was over.

She was gone.

I stood there, my gloves still on, the sterile drapes around her body crumpled in disarray. The monitors had gone silent, their blank screens a stark reminder of the life that had slipped away. Around me, the team moved quietly, packing up instruments, cleaning the room. Their faces betrayed no emotion—they had done this before.

But I hadn't.

I left the OR and found myself wandering the halls, still in my scrubs, the smell of antiseptic clinging to me. I passed the patient's son in the waiting room. He stood as I approached, his eyes wide with hope and fear.

"How is she?" he asked, his voice cracking.

I froze, the words catching in my throat. There is no class in medical school, no lecture, no textbook that prepares you for this moment. For the look in a family member's eyes when you tell them you couldn't save the person they loved.

"I'm so sorry," I managed to say. "We did everything we could."

He stared at me, uncomprehending. Then, as the meaning of my words sank in, he crumpled, his body folding in on itself. I reached out to steady him, but he shrugged me off, his grief too raw, too overwhelming for comfort.

I walked away, my legs trembling, my chest tight.

That night, I sat alone in my small apartment, replaying every moment of the surgery in my mind. I thought about the incision, the positioning, the instruments I'd used. Had I missed something? Had I moved too quickly? Too slowly? The weight of the loss settled on my shoulders, heavy and suffocating.

I didn't sleep.

Over the next few days, I carried the grief with me like an open wound. It colored everything I did, every decision I made. I saw her face in every patient, heard her son's voice in every anxious family member. I doubted myself in ways I

never had before.

It took weeks, months even, to find some semblance of acceptance. To understand that her death wasn't my fault, that sometimes, despite our best efforts, the body fails in ways we can't predict or control.

But the truth is, the grief never really goes away. It becomes a part of you, woven into the fabric of who you are as a surgeon and as a person.

Now, when I stand in the OR, I carry her memory with me. Not as a shadow, but as a reminder. A reminder of the weight of this work, of the trust patients place in us, and of the fragility of life.

Every surgeon has their first loss. It's a rite of passage, a grim initiation into the reality of this profession. And though it breaks something inside you, it also builds

something new—a deeper respect for the patients who trust
you, a sharper awareness of your limits, and an unshakable resolve to do better.
Her name was Mrs. Mehta. I will never forget her.

CHAPTER THREE

THE BREAKING POINT

It was supposed to be a straightforward procedure. A tibial plateau fracture—severe, but not unmanageable. I had done my pre-op planning meticulously, rehearsed every step in my mind. The patient, a 32-year-old construction worker, had slipped from scaffolding, his knee crumpling under the weight of the fall. He'd come to me hoping to avoid a lifelong limp, trusting me with his future. We started the case mid-afternoon, and the hours stretched on as they often do in orthopedics. The fracture was more complex than the imaging had suggested. The bones were shattered like a jigsaw puzzle, tiny fragments teasingly close but maddeningly out of alignment. Each attempt to piece them together felt like trying to sculpt with

sand.

"Another millimeter," I muttered to myself, knowing that even a slight imperfection could affect the patient's mobility. The scrub nurse handed me another clamp without a word—her quiet efficiency a small comfort in the chaos.

By hour four, my confidence began to falter. My hands, usually steady, felt leaden. The C-arm monitor blurred as fatigue set in. I adjusted the fluoroscope again, hoping for clarity, but the fragments seemed to mock me, slipping out of place the moment I thought I had them secured.

"Let's take a five-minute pause," I said, stepping back from the table. My voice was calm, but inside, I was unravelling.

I leaned against the wall of the OR, my mask hiding the exhaustion etched across my face. The resident, a sharpeyed

second-year, looked at me expectantly, waiting for instructions I wasn't sure I could give. The patient's life wasn't in danger, but his future—his ability to work, to run, to live without pain—hung in the balance.

A voice in my head whispered the truth I didn't want to face: You're not good enough for this.

Surgeons aren't supposed to feel this way. We're trained to be decisive, unshakable. But in that moment, I felt like an imposter, standing in a room filled with people who expected me to fix what felt unfixable.

I thought about calling for help—asking my senior colleague to step in. But pride, or perhaps fear, stopped me. What if they saw my failure? What if they confirmed the doubt gnawing at me?

Instead, I took a breath, pushed away the doubt, and returned to the table. The next hour passed in a haze of clamps, screws, and silent prayers. When the final screw was in place and the fragments aligned as best they could be, I stepped back and let the resident close.

It wasn't perfect. I knew that. The post-op films would show slight imperfections, deviations I would see every time I thought of the case. But the patient would walk again, and for now, that was enough.

I stayed late that night, long after the OR lights dimmed and the halls grew quiet. In the stillness of my office, I finally allowed myself to feel the weight of the day. I thought about how easily we expect ourselves to carry these burdens alone, how rarely we admit when we're at our limits.

The truth is, surgery isn't just about skill or precision. It's about endurance—of the body, yes, but also of the mind. It's

about knowing when to push through and when to ask for help.

I didn't call for help that day, and I'm not sure if that was courage or foolishness. But I learned something important: there is no shame in admitting you're human.

The next day, I walked into the OR again. The doubt was still there, lingering in the shadows, but so was the determination. I knew the breaking point wasn't a failure— it was a lesson. One that I would carry with me, like all the scars we surgeons collect, visible or not.

CHAPTER FOUR

THE PERFECT PATIENT

Every surgeon has a patient who lingers in their
memory, not because of the complexity of the
procedure but because of the storm of emotions
they bring with them. For me, it was Mrs. Gupta.
She arrived in my clinic on a humid July afternoon,
clutching an oversized handbag and wearing an expression
that immediately set me on edge. Her gait was stiff, her
knee clearly failing her, yet her sharp eyes scanned the
room as if searching for faults.

"I've been to five doctors already," she announced as she
sat down, her voice carrying an air of challenge. "No one
has helped me."

Her MRI confirmed the obvious: advanced osteoarthritis
in her right knee. The cartilage was gone, bone grinding
against bone with every step she took. A total knee
replacement was the only logical solution. But logic wasn't
Mrs. Gupta's strong suit, as I quickly learned.

"I've read that implants fail," she said, her tone
suspicious. "I don't want some cheap, experimental
device."

"We use the best implants available," I assured her. "They're reliable and have excellent outcomes."

She wasn't convinced. "And the surgery? I've heard it's risky. Someone I know got an infection and couldn't walk again."

Her skepticism was exhausting, but I knew it wasn't entirely misplaced. Surgery is never without risk, and patients like Mrs. Gupta, who have combed through every worst-case scenario on the internet, are often the hardest to reassure.

"What would you like to do?" I asked, hoping to shift the responsibility back to her.

She crossed her arms. "I want my knee to be fixed, but I don't want surgery."

It was one of those moments where I had to take a deep breath and remind myself of the fundamental truth of medicine: behind every difficult patient is a person afraid of
losing control.

Over the next few weeks, she tested my patience to its limits. She questioned every decision, argued about every recommendation, and even brought her son—an engineer who suddenly fancied himself an expert in orthopedics—to interrogate me during one consultation.

And yet, there was something about Mrs. Gupta that kept me from writing her off entirely. Beneath her combative exterior was a woman deeply afraid of what the future held. She had lost her husband to a heart attack just a year earlier, and her world had shrunk to the walls of her apartment and the painful steps she took between them. When she finally agreed to the surgery, it felt like a small miracle. I scheduled her for a total knee replacement, determined to prove that her fears, while valid, were not inevitable.

In the operating room, everything went smoothly. The implant fit perfectly, the alignment was flawless, and as I closed the incision, I felt a rare sense of satisfaction.

Mrs. Gupta's recovery was slow, as I expected it to be, but every milestone felt like a victory. The first time she walked with a walker. The first time she managed a flight of stairs. The first time she smiled at me during a follow-up appointment instead of glaring.

"You've done a good job," she said grudgingly after six months, her tone almost approving.

It wasn't until a year later, when she came back for her final check-up, that I saw the full transformation. She walked into my clinic unassisted, her steps firm and confident. She talked about visiting her grandchildren, about the market trips she had resumed, about feeling like herself again.

"Thank you," she said, her voice softer than I had ever heard it.

In that moment, I realized something humbling: Mrs. Gupta wasn't a perfect patient, but she had taught me lessons I didn't know I needed. She forced me to confront my own biases, to see past the frustration and remember that trust isn't always given freely—it's earned.

Medicine is full of patients like Mrs. Gupta, people who test us, challenge us, and sometimes leave us questioning why we chose this profession at all. But they're also the ones who remind us of the power of perseverance, of listening, of meeting fear with compassion.

She may not have been the patient I wanted, but she was exactly the one I needed.

CHAPTER FIVE

THE EXPERIMENT

In rorthopedics, time is both an ally and an adversary. Knees, in particular, are like machines—they endure decades of wear before parts start to grind, crack, and finally fail. The decision we face as surgeons is whether to intervene early and attempt repair, knowing the outcome may be uncertain, or wait, letting the damage accumulate until replacement is the only option.

The patient sitting before me was the embodiment of that dilemma. Prakash, 47, a schoolteacher, had been struggling with knee pain for years. His cartilage was frayed but not yet gone, the subchondral bone below peeking through like roots exposed beneath thinning soil.

"I can still walk," he said, wincing slightly as he shifted in his chair. "But stairs are difficult, and I can't keep up with the children at school anymore. They run ahead, and I just... watch."

He had tried physiotherapy, braces, and injections, each offering a temporary reprieve but never a cure. Now, the question was simple in its phrasing but fraught with complexity: repair or wait?

Repair meant an experimental cartilage regeneration procedure. It was a chance to slow the clock, to rebuild the damaged tissue and give him years of relief before a knee replacement became inevitable. But the procedure came with caveats—variable success rates, a long recovery, and the risk of failure that might even hasten his decline. Waiting, on the other hand, meant pain. It meant watching his mobility slowly erode, waiting for the day when his knee would be bad enough to justify a replacement. A total knee arthroplasty was predictable, reliable, and proven—but it came with its own price. At 47, he would likely outlive the implant, requiring revision surgeries in the future.

"What would you do, Doctor?" he asked, his question cutting through the clinical explanations I had rehearsed.

I paused, weighing my response. What would I do?

On one hand, I believed in progress. The repair was part of a cutting-edge trial, and early results were promising. If it

worked, it could redefine his life—preserving his joint, his mobility, his ability to chase after his students. But I also knew the uncertainty. Experimental procedures are a gamble, and Prakash wasn't just a statistic in a trial; he was a person, a teacher, a father.

On the other hand, waiting seemed pragmatic. Let the natural course of degeneration run until replacement became the clear solution. But it also felt like surrender, like asking him to endure years of pain when there was a chance, however slim, to offer him something better.

In the end, Prakash chose repair.

The surgery was meticulous. I harvested his cells, cultivated them in a lab, and returned weeks later to implant a delicate scaffold of regenerated cartilage into his knee. As I sutured the incision, I thought about the duality of what we had done—offering both hope and risk.

His recovery was slow, as expected, but steady. Each follow-up brought cautious optimism. By six months, he was walking without pain. By a year, he was climbing stairs, even jogging lightly in the park.

But medicine has a way of tempering triumph with reality. At 18 months, he came back with a familiar stiffness.

The MRI showed some wear on the new cartilage—not a failure, but not the unqualified success I had hoped for either.

Still, Prakash smiled. "It's better than it was," he said. "I can keep up with my students now. That's enough for me."

His words stayed with me. Success in medicine isn't always about perfection. Sometimes, it's about buying time, about giving someone a reprieve that lets them live a little fuller, a little longer.

The decision between repair and replacement isn't a question of right or wrong; it's a question of priorities. Do we gamble on progress, knowing the risks, or wait for certainty, knowing the cost of delay?

For Prakash, the experiment worked—not flawlessly, but meaningfully. And perhaps that's the best we can hope for in this balancing act between science and humanity: to offer something better, even if it's not perfect.

CHAPTER SIX

THE HIDDEN CURRICULUM

The operating room teaches you things that no textbook ever could. It's a place where sterility reigns but chaos is never far away, where seconds stretch into hours and decisions can shape the arc of a life—or end it.

No one tells you how to manage the silence that follows a misstep, the kind that drowns out the hum of the monitors and makes the weight of your gown feel unbearable. No one explains the creeping self-doubt that comes after a complication, the whispers in your head that question your skill, your judgment, your very place in this field.

These are lessons I learned not from mentors or textbooks, but from patients.

Take Ravi, for instance. He was a 45-year-old businessman who came to me with relentless knee pain. His joint had been worn down to a nub by years of untreated arthritis, and every step he took was a grimaceinducing struggle. He was a textbook candidate for a total knee replacement—routine, by all accounts.

The surgery was smooth, almost disappointingly so. The cuts were clean, the implant aligned perfectly. As I closed the wound, I felt that fleeting moment of satisfaction, the kind that makes you believe, for just a second, that you've mastered the art of surgery.

But two days later, Ravi's leg swelled alarmingly. His pain, which should have lessened, spiked. The diagnosis was quick and cruel: a postoperative infection. A rare complication, they said. The kind of thing you read about in case studies, the numbers too small to scare you. Until it's your patient.

I spent sleepless nights rethinking every step of the surgery. Had I missed something? Was the drape not properly secured? Did I hesitate too long when tying a suture? The guilt felt corrosive, like acid dripping onto my confidence.

The infection required another surgery, this time to debride the wound. I explained this to Ravi as gently as I could, but he simply nodded, his face betraying no emotion. It was almost worse than anger; I would have welcomed his rage, his shouting. Instead, his calm acceptance felt like forgiveness I didn't deserve.

The second surgery went well, and over the weeks that followed, Ravi improved. But the experience left a scar on me as well as him. It was a harsh reminder that even in a well-practiced procedure, you're never entirely in control.

Then there was Meera, a 63-year-old grandmother who had been bedridden for months with a severe valgus deformity. Her knees had bowed outward so severely that walking was impossible. The first time I met her, she clasped my hands in hers and said, "Doctor, I just want to dance at my granddaughter's wedding."

Her surgery was far from routine. Years of deformity had

left her ligaments stretched thin and her bones warped. I spent hours planning, rehearsing each step in my head. In the OR, I worked methodically, cutting away the damaged bone, fitting the implant like a puzzle piece.

When it was done, I felt a surge of pride—a rare emotion in a profession where self-congratulation is a dangerous luxury. Meera's recovery was remarkable. Within weeks, she was walking, her face alight with joy. She did dance at that wedding, and she sent me a video—a grainy clip that I still watch on my worst days, a reminder of why I chose this path.

These moments—Ravi's infection, Meera's triumph—are part of the hidden curriculum of surgery. They teach you resilience, but not in the way you'd expect. Resilience isn't about brushing off failure or ignoring the weight of your mistakes. It's about carrying that weight, letting it shape you without letting it crush you.

And then there's the lesson you learn last: how to let go. Surgery demands control, precision, mastery. But life, as it turns out, doesn't follow such rules. Sometimes, despite your best efforts, outcomes are dictated by forces you cannot predict or prevent.

In the end, the operating room is less about perfection than it is about persistence. The unrelenting pressure, the unpredictable outcomes, the patients who teach you what no mentor ever could—this is the hidden curriculum. It's not in the textbooks or the lectures. It's written in the silence of the OR, the weight of a patient's trust, and the quiet moments when you realize you're still learning, every single day.

CHAPTER SEVEN

THE GREY ZONE

The morning had started like any other. Rounds, charts, the obligatory coffee that was always lukewarm by the time I got to it. Yet, by midday, I found myself staring at a case that would pull me into the murky waters of what we euphemistically call "the gray zone."

The patient was Mr. Dutta, a 72-year-old retired teacher who had once walked five kilometers a day but was now confined to a hospital bed, his left knee swollen to twice its size, grotesquely deformed. The X-rays were devastating: advanced osteoarthritis compounded by a poorly healed fracture from years ago. His blood work whispered of other complications—chronic kidney disease and borderline diabetes.

It wasn't the first time I'd seen a case like his. But the difference here wasn't just the physical complexity; it was the fact that Mr. Dutta's condition teetered on the edge of what surgery could achieve.

His son, a wiry man in his thirties, met me in the corridor outside the ward. "Doctor, please," he began, his voice trembling with a mix of urgency and exhaustion. "You have to help him. He can't live like this anymore."

Inside, Mr. Dutta sat propped up on pillows, his breathing shallow. Despite the pain that etched itself onto his face, his eyes were bright, watchful. "Doctor," he said softly, "what do you think? Should I do this?"

I paused, weighing my words carefully.

A total knee replacement could restore mobility and alleviate his pain. It could also trigger a cascade of complications—cardiac strain, delayed wound healing, or worse, a kidney crisis. The safest option was conservative management: pain relief, physiotherapy, and lifestyle adjustments. Yet, I knew what that meant for someone like him—a slow surrender to immobility.

"Your knees are not just joints," I finally said. "They're a part of how you've lived your life. This isn't just about surgery; it's about what you want your life to look like from here."

He nodded, his gaze dropping to his hands. "I want to walk again," he said. "I want to go to the market, sit on the park bench with my friends. I'm not asking for much, Doctor. Just to be able to live."

It was moments like this that made me envy the simplicity of numbers and scans, the cold objectivity of data. None of it accounted for the weight of a person's desire, the intangible force of hope.

I explained the risks to both father and son, laying out the potential for complications as honestly as I could. Mr. Dutta listened, occasionally glancing at his son, who sat silently, his jaw set in determination.

Finally, the son spoke. "If you think it's possible, Doctor, we'll take the risk."

I excused myself to think. To retreat into the safety of my office, where I could pace and deliberate. What tipped the balance wasn't the X-rays or lab reports—it was the image of

Mr. Dutta sitting in that bed, his hands resting on his lap as if bracing himself for life's final indignity.

The surgery was set for the following week.

The operation itself was grueling. The bone was brittle, the deformity severe, and my own doubt whispered at the edges of my focus. But with every measured cut, every careful adjustment, I felt the resolve that had brought me here. My hands moved with the precision born of repetition, but my mind hovered in that gray zone, questioning, second-guessing.

When I stepped out of the OR hours later, my scrubs soaked and my shoulders aching, I found the son waiting. "It went well," I said. His face lit up with gratitude, but my own relief was tempered by the long road ahead.

Weeks later, Mr. Dutta returned to my clinic for his first post-op check-up. He walked in with the help of a cane, each step slow but deliberate. His son trailed behind, smiling broadly.

"How does it feel?" I asked.

Mr. Dutta looked down at his new knee, then back up at me. "Like I've been given another chance," he said.

The gray zone is where we live most of our professional lives—not in the stark black-and-white certainty of right or wrong, but in the messy, uncertain middle. It's where science meets humanity, where every decision carries the weight of its consequences.

That day, as Mr. Dutta left the clinic, I watched him navigate the hallway with cautious confidence. He was no longer just a patient with a fractured joint or a failing body. He was a man reclaiming his life, one uncertain step at a time.

And for that moment, the gray zone felt like the only

place I wanted to be.

CHAPTER EIGHT

THE HANDS WE TRUST

Surgeries usually begin with a symphony of
certainty. Instruments gleaming under the harsh
glare of the overhead light, monitors humming with
reassuring regularity, and a team moving in seamless
synchrony, each member knowing their role as if
choreographed. But today, something was different.
The patient was a 54-year-old farmer, Mr. Rajan, who had
been struggling with severe arthritis for years. He'd come
to
us after exhausting every possible remedy: herbal oils,
temple visits, even a local bone-setter who had promised a
miracle cure but left him worse off than before. A total
knee
replacement was his last hope, and I had assured him that
he was in good hands.
The case started like any other. The spinal anesthesia had
taken effect, the monitors were stable, and the instruments
gleamed under the bright OR lights. I made the first
incision, careful and deliberate, peeling back layers of skin
and muscle to expose the joint. Everything was going as

planned until I reached for the oscillating saw to begin cutting through the bone.

It didn't turn on.

"Try again," I said, my voice calm, though a flicker of unease began to creep in.

The scrub nurse adjusted the connections and handed it back. I pressed the trigger. Nothing.

"The power's fine," the anesthetist said, glancing at the wall sockets.

"It's the saw," the nurse murmured, her voice tense. "It's not responding."

A quick flurry of activity followed as the team scrambled to check the backup. But the backup wasn't working either. Some electrical issue, they concluded. The hospital's aging equipment had failed us.

I took a deep breath, trying to quell the rising wave of frustration. This wasn't just inconvenient—it was dangerous. Prolonged surgeries increase the risk of complications: infection, blood loss, even anesthesiarelated issues. And here we were, stuck.

"We'll need to do this manually," I said finally, locking eyes with the senior scrub nurse. She nodded, understanding immediately what it meant.

She handed me the manual bone saw—a tool that hadn't seen regular use in years. It was heavier, less precise, and far more demanding of the surgeon's hand. In a world of modern gadgets and robotic-assisted procedures, it felt like stepping back into an era where outcomes depended entirely on the steadiness of your grip and the sharpness of your focus.

I positioned the blade and began sawing, the resistance of the bone sending vibrations up my arm. The room fell silent, except for the sound of metal on bone and the steady beep of the monitors. My team adjusted seamlessly, anticipating my every need. The scrub nurse handed me instruments before I even asked. The anesthetist kept a close eye on the patient's vitals, her voice steady as she updated me.

Time seemed to stretch and compress all at once. My muscles ached from the strain, sweat trickled down my back despite the cool temperature of the room, and my mind raced to double-check every step. There was no margin for error—not with this tool, not under these conditions.

Finally, the cut was complete. I took a moment to flex my fingers, now stiff from the effort, and moved on to positioning the implant. Piece by piece, the joint came together, the prosthesis fitting into place as if it were made for him—which, in a way, it was.

By the time we closed the incision, the monitors told me we'd been in the OR far longer than I'd planned. But Mr. Rajan was stable, his new knee in place, and the room began to buzz with the relief of a team that had just weathered a storm together.

Later, as I sat in the locker room peeling off my gloves, I thought about how reliant we've become on technology. It makes us faster, more efficient, more precise. But today had been a stark reminder of what lies beneath all of that: the hands we trust.

Hands that can adapt when machines fail. Hands that can steady a trembling heart or repair a shattered bone. Hands that carry the weight of human lives every single day.

It wasn't a perfect surgery—not by the standards of modern operating rooms—but it was a testament to what can happen when skill, intuition, and teamwork come together.

The next morning, I checked on Mr. Rajan. He was propped up in bed, his leg encased in a brace, his eyes shining with relief and hope.

"Thank you, Doctor," he said simply, folding his hands in gratitude.

I smiled, the soreness in my arms suddenly inconsequential. Sometimes, the best outcomes come not from the tools we use, but from the hands—and the hearts—

that guide them.

CHAPTER NINE

THE SILENT HELPERS

The room was sterile, the lights too bright, the tension palpable. My hands moved automatically, part of a routine I had performed countless times before. But something felt different today. Maybe it was the way the patient's leg lay on the table, the unusual angle, or the persistent thought in my mind that I hadn't given enough attention to the people who made all this possible. It's easy, when you're standing in the center of the operating room, to believe the success of a procedure rests entirely in your hands. The surgeon is the one who holds the scalpel, the one who makes the final call. The patient's life, their future mobility, is in your hands. But that's an illusion, a dangerous myth. The truth is, no surgery is ever truly solo. Not the way it appears on paper, not the way it seems in your head.

"Can you get me a smaller retractor?" I ask, my voice hoarse despite the sterile mask. Priya, the scrub nurse, is already moving before the words fully leave my mouth. I don't have to ask twice; I don't even have to look up. She's anticipated my needs.

I watch her hands, steady and graceful, as she works. She doesn't speak much, doesn't seek recognition, but every move she makes is like poetry in motion. The retractor is in my hand before I can finish my thought, positioned exactly as I need it. She's seen this surgery a hundred times, but today it's different. Today I feel the weight of her presence more than ever.

"Angle's off by a few degrees," I mutter, more to myself than to anyone else. Ravi, the radiology technician, doesn't miss a beat. He's already adjusting the fluoroscope, the image on the screen flickering and stabilizing as he finetunes

it with quiet precision. His job is simple in theory: to capture the images I need. But when something goes wrong —when a fracture doesn't quite line up or a screw doesn't thread the way it should—Ravi is the one who fixes it before

I even have the chance to realize there's a problem.

The hum of machines, the sound of monitors beeping, the soft shuffle of feet—these are the noises I associate with surgery. But there's another sound, one I don't often acknowledge, though it's always there: the silence of the people who work just as hard as I do. The ones who never take center stage, but whose work is what keeps the whole machine running smoothly.

Outside the OR, the cleaning staff is already preparing for the next round of surgeries. Sanjay, who never complains, who always has a smile for me even when I'm too busy to acknowledge him, is somewhere down the hall, mopping the floors, scrubbing away the evidence of yesterday's work. He's here before I am, and he stays long after I've gone home. No one thanks him, no one notices the small but vital role he plays in this entire process. But without him, there would be no room for us to work in. No sterile field, no clean space.

Sometimes, I catch myself thinking that surgery is about individual brilliance. About the surgeon—the one in the sterile gown—who makes the cut, the one who decides. But that's not how it is. Not really. Every successful surgery is a product of hundreds of small acts, each one as crucial as the last. From the nurse who checks the supplies, to the anesthetist who ensures the patient's stability, to the technician who monitors the imaging, to the cleaning staff who keep the environment safe.

Today, as I finish the last stitch and step back to admire the neat closure, I feel something unfamiliar. Gratitude. Not for the surgery I just performed, but for those who made it possible. For Priya, for Ravi, for Sanjay, for the dozens of unseen hands that worked in unison to ensure the patient's safety.

We never stop to acknowledge them, not really. In the fast-paced world of surgery, there's no time for thanks, no time to reflect. But today, as I look around the room, I realize how much I owe them. How much we all owe them. Without them, there is no success, no healing.

And in the stillness of the moment, after the patient is wheeled away and the room begins to empty, I feel a quiet reverence for those whose contributions go unnoticed. For the silent helpers who are as much a part of the healing process as the surgeon at the table.

As I wash my hands, the hum of the operating room fading behind me, I think of them, and for the first time, I give thanks. Not just for the patient whose knee is now stable, but for the people who helped make it happen. They are the unsung heroes of this work, the ones who never wear the title of savior—but who, in the quiet spaces, are the ones who truly carry the load.

CHAPTER TEN

THE PATIENT WHO CHANGED EVERYTHING

The day began like any other—predictable in its chaos, a string of routine knee replacements and follow-ups. By midday, my thoughts were already veering toward lunch, a rare indulgence in the world of orthopedic surgery. That's when they wheeled her in: a petite woman in her late twenties, her leg twisted in a grotesque angle that defied anatomy.

"Road accident," the ER resident briefed me. "Compound fracture, tibial plateau. But there's more." There was always more. In my years of practice, I'd learned that patients rarely presented as textbook cases. Yet, as I peeled back the sterile drapes to examine her, I felt a twinge of unease—not just because of the severity of the injury, but because something about it didn't add up.

Her knee was swollen to twice its size, the skin stretched taut, shiny. The X-rays revealed not just a shattered tibial plateau, but tiny fragments that had scattered like shrapnel, as if her bone had imploded rather than fractured. But it wasn't the mechanics of the injury that troubled me. It was the infection—a putrid, greenish fluid oozing from the wound, its smell unmistakable.

"How long ago did the accident happen?" I asked the resident, though I already knew the answer wasn't going to satisfy me.

"Two weeks."

Two weeks. The words hung in the air, heavy with implications. She'd spent fourteen days at a district hospital, her wound festering while they tried and failed to stabilize her leg. By the time her family had scraped together the money and the courage to transfer her to the city, the infection had a head start we could never hope to match.

"We'll debride and stabilize the fracture," I said, more to myself than to anyone in the room. The resident nodded, his face carefully neutral.

As we prepared for surgery, I couldn't shake the feeling that I was missing something. Infections after open fractures were common enough, but this one felt... different. Aggressive. Almost sentient in its destruction. The fragments of bone seemed to be dissolving before my eyes, their edges jagged and porous in a way I hadn't seen before. The surgery itself was uneventful, if such a word could be used for a case like this. We removed as much of the necrotic tissue as we could, cleaned out the infection, and stabilized the fracture with an external fixator. It was a patchwork solution, a desperate bid to buy her some time. But as the days turned into weeks, it became clear that time wasn't on her side. The infection spread, defying every antibiotic we threw at it. Cultures came back negative, adding to the mystery. I pored over her charts, reexamined

her imaging, even called in colleagues from other specialties, but no one had answers.

Her condition deteriorated, and with it, my confidence. Every time I walked into her room, I was met with her unwavering gaze—a mix of trust and expectation that made my chest tighten. She believed in me, even as I began to doubt myself.

It was during one of those visits that she asked, "Will I walk again?"

I hesitated. The truth sat like a stone in my throat, unspoken but undeniable. "We're doing everything we can," I said finally. It wasn't a lie, but it wasn't the answer she deserved.

One evening, long after the hospital had settled into its nightly rhythm of hushed footsteps and muted monitors, I found myself back in her room. Her family had gone home for the night, leaving her alone with her thoughts and the incessant hum of the IV pump.

"I've been thinking," she said, her voice barely above a whisper. "Even if you can't save my leg, you've saved my life. That's enough."

I stared at her, startled by her clarity. Here was a young woman who had every reason to rage against the injustice of her circumstances, yet she was comforting me.

In the end, we couldn't save her leg. The infection was too entrenched, the damage too extensive. Amputation was the only option, a decision that felt like a personal failure despite its inevitability. But she survived, and in the months that followed, she returned to the hospital, first for fittings for her prosthetic, then just to visit.

She became a kind of fixture in our ward, her resilience a

quiet inspiration to patients and staff alike. She taught me something that no textbook or surgical manual ever could: that medicine is as much about humility as it is about skill. Not every story ends with a triumphant return to normalcy. But sometimes, survival itself is the victory, and the courage to adapt is what changes everything. For her, it meant learning to live with one leg. For me, it meant learning to accept the limits of what I could do, and finding grace in the effort.

She walked into my clinic one day, her prosthetic barely noticeable under a long skirt. "I wanted to thank you," she said simply.

"No," I replied, my voice catching. "It's I who should thank you."

CHAPTER ELEVEN

THE FIRST CUT

The sterile smell of the operating room was a
constant companion, a scent that clung to my
scrubs, my gloves, and my conscience. My fingers
felt slick as I fumbled for the scalpel, the cold steel heavier
than I had ever imagined. I had spent years learning
anatomy, memorizing surgical techniques, and watching
countless procedures, but none of that prepared me for the
reality of it—the weight of responsibility, the magnitude of
the moment when the incision is made, and there's no
turning back.

"Are you ready?" Dr. Kim's voice sliced through the
tension in the room.

I nodded, though inside I felt anything but ready. My
heart was pounding in my chest, and my palms were
sweaty, despite the coolness of the operating room. This
was it—the first time I would be leading a surgery,
performing the procedure from start to finish. The patient,
an elderly man whose knee had deteriorated to the point of
near immobility, had put his trust in me, and I could feel
that trust pressing down on my shoulders, heavy as stone.

"Remember, the key is confidence," Dr. Kim continued,
his voice calm, authoritative. "Even when you're unsure,

act with conviction. If you hesitate, your hands will hesitate."

I forced myself to take a deep breath, my gaze flickering over to the patient's knee. The problem was clear: osteoarthritis had eaten away at the joint, leaving bone on bone. But now, I was the one who would be responsible for putting things right. The incision would be the first step, and in that moment, it felt like the most important step of my life.

I took the scalpel, its weight familiar but alien in my trembling hands, and with a steady motion, I made the incision. A small, deliberate cut through the skin, the beginning of the transformation. It wasn't perfect, but it was clean. Dr. Kim nodded approvingly from behind me. The next steps—dissecting tissues, exposing the joint—were

a blur. I moved as I had been trained, but the internal dissonance between my training and my nerves was deafening.

"Good," Dr. Kim said, watching carefully as I worked. "The key to success is in the details, the small things—how you handle the tissues, how you manage bleeding, how you prepare for the unexpected."

I nodded, though my mind was anything but calm. The procedure continued, each motion becoming more automatic, but with every step, the gravity of what I was doing seemed to grow. This wasn't just about fixing a knee—

it was about restoring a life. Mobility was everything to this patient. He had worked his whole life as a farmer, relying on his body to sustain him. This knee, once a tool of his livelihood, had betrayed him, and now I was here, a young surgeon, to set it right.

But what if I failed? What if the ligament I was about to repair didn't hold? What if, instead of restoring his life, I left him worse than before? The questions buzzed in my head, but I forced them back, focusing on the task at hand. The procedure ended without incident. The joint was repaired, the knee stable, and I had successfully navigated my first major surgery. But as I stood in the post-op room, looking at the closed incision, I realized something I hadn't expected. The true challenge wasn't the procedure—it was what came next. The follow-up. The healing. The uncertainty of knowing whether my work would last, whether I would have done enough.

Dr. Kim clapped me on the back as we walked out of the OR, his tone light. "You did well today. A good first step." But I could hear the underlying message in his voice. A surgeon is never defined by one operation. It's the cumulative result, the ongoing effort to improve, to learn from every case, that makes us who we are.

As I made my way back to the residents' lounge, I couldn't shake the feeling that the weight of the scalpel would stay with me long after the stitches had been tied. Each patient, each procedure, would bring new challenges, new opportunities for mistakes. And in those moments, I would have to learn not just how to fix bodies, but how to fix myself—how to trust myself, how to live with the pressure of knowing that every cut I made had consequences.

Because in surgery, there are no true do-overs. Every incision is final. And so, the learning curve begins—not just with the skills, but with the awareness that as surgeons, we are always evolving, always learning, and always striving for perfection—one incision at a time.

CHAPTER TWELVE

MINIMAL INVASIVE SURGERY

The knee is a deceptively simple structure. It bends, it straightens, it bears our weight, and we barely notice it—until it stops working. Then, it becomes a tyrant. A twinge here, a sharp pain there, until every step feels like betrayal. It's strange to think that something so small—a worn patch of cartilage, a torn ligament—can bring a person's world to a standstill.

As a knee surgeon, I've seen how the pain of a failing joint doesn't just rob people of their mobility; it steals their identity. The runner who can no longer run. The grandparent unable to kneel and play with their grandchildren. They arrive in my clinic, clutching X-rays and MRIs, desperate for relief. For years, the answer often came with a heavy price—an open incision, weeks of recovery, months of rehab. But today, there's a new way. Minimally invasive surgery. The words are almost too smooth, too simple for what they promise. Tiny incisions, shorter hospital stays, a faster return to life. It sounds like a miracle, doesn't it? And in many ways, it is. But as with all miracles in medicine, it comes with its own complexities and a steep learning curve.

I remember the first time I performed a minimally invasive multi ligament injury of knee. It felt unnatural, almost counterintuitive, to work through such a small incision. The instruments felt awkward in my hands, the field of view limited to what the camera showed on the screen. My instincts, honed through years of open surgery, screamed for a wider view, a better angle. But I persisted, learning to trust the tools and the process. Slowly, I began to see the potential.

Now, I can't imagine practicing any other way. Minimally invasive knee surgery is both an art and a science. Instead of a long incision down the center of the knee, we use small portals, each barely a few centimeters wide. A camera, no bigger than a pen, provides a magnified view of the joint's intricate anatomy. Instruments designed for precision navigate the confined space, shaving away damaged cartilage or stitching torn ligaments with delicate movements.

For a torn meniscus, what used to require a long incision and weeks of recovery can now be done arthroscopically in under an hour. Even total knee replacements—once considered the realm of open surgery—have been transformed. Through advanced navigation systems and robotics, we can align and place implants with an accuracy that the naked eye could never achieve.

Patients are often astonished when I explain the process. They imagine surgery as a brutal, invasive ordeal. "You mean you don't have to open the whole knee?" they ask, disbelief mingled with hope. I explain the advantages: less pain, less blood loss, a shorter stay in the hospital, and a quicker recovery. Most are walking with assistance the very next day.

But it's not just the physical recovery that changes—it's the emotional one, too. A smaller scar, barely noticeable after a few months, doesn't just mark the body less; it marks the mind less. It's easier to move on, to forget the trauma, to simply live again.

Of course, minimally invasive surgery is not without its challenges. The narrow field of view means that every movement must be deliberate, every decision precise.

There is no room for error. Unlike open surgery, where you can see and feel the anatomy directly, MIS relies on your understanding of anatomy, your training, and your trust in the technology.

There are times when the instruments seem to have a mind of their own, slipping where you don't want them to, or when the anatomy doesn't look like it should—scar tissue

from an old injury, or a joint so riddled with arthritis that the usual landmarks are unrecognizable. These moments test your patience and your skill, reminding you that no matter how advanced the tools, surgery is still a human endeavor.

A Step into the Future

And yet, despite its challenges, minimally invasive knee surgery represents the future. Robotics, augmented reality, and advanced imaging are pushing the boundaries of what we can achieve. Someday, we may even be able to regenerate cartilage or replace joints entirely without making a single incision.

But for now, the tools we have are enough to change lives. To take someone who has been living in pain, watching their world shrink with every step, and give them back not just their mobility, but their sense of self—that is the true power of minimally invasive surgery.

As a knee surgeon, I still marvel at the elegance of it. To see a joint in high definition, to work with instruments that seem to merge with your hands, to close a surgery with stitches so small they disappear in weeks—it is nothing short of extraordinary.

And yet, as I watch a patient walk out of my clinic, their stride steady and their smile returning, I am reminded that the true miracle lies not in the tools or the techniques, but in the resilience of the human body and spirit. A resilience that we, as surgeons, have the privilege to restore.